In the Days of the Dinosaurs

The Asteroid

Story by Hugh Price and Beverley Randell

Illustrations by Ben Spiby

NELSON PRICE MILBURN

Long, long ago, in the age of the dinosaurs,
Tor lived in a forest.
She was a little furry mammal with a tail,
and she was not much bigger than a mouse.
Tor had claws for climbing trees.
She had a long nose,
and large eyes that saw well in the dark.

At night, when the dinosaurs slept,
Tor and her troop hurried about.
They ate the insects that hid in the trees,
and other little creatures
that crawled on the forest floor.

The dinosaurs were all much, much larger
than the little mammals.
If the mammals heard a dinosaur coming,
they fled!
Tyrannosaurus Rex was a thousand times
heavier than they were!

Tor was going to have some babies.
They were growing inside her
where they were warm and safe.

When it was time for them to be born,
Tor found a hole inside a fallen tree.
There she made a warm nest,
and when her babies were born
she fed them with her milk.

The dinosaurs did not give birth to babies.
They laid eggs instead.
Dinosaur eggs could not hatch
unless they were warmed by the hot sun.

The huge dinosaurs were busy in the daytime,
and the tiny mammals were busy at night,
as they had been for millions of years.

Then, suddenly,
the world changed forever!

A huge white-hot ball of burning rock
roared down from the sky.
It was an asteroid.

The asteroid hit the ground at great speed
and exploded.
It made an enormous crater in the earth.
Rocks melted in the heat.
Giant clouds of gas and smoke and dust
were thrown high into the sky.
Thousands of trees caught fire
and all living things near the crater died.

The thick dark clouds of gas and dust
drifted right around the earth.

Tor lived on the other side of the world.
Her forest was far from the crater,
but even so, clouds piled up
and hid the sun.
The sunlight could not break through.

In the weeks and months and years
that followed the explosion,
most days were grey and cold
all over the world.

But what did cold days matter to Tor
and other furry mammals
who had always gone hunting in the dark?
They had fur to keep them warm.
And they still fed on tiny creatures
in the trees and on the forest floor.

Soon Tor had some more babies
growing safely inside her.
She made another nest,
and after they were born
she fed them with her warm milk.

Tor and most of her babies stayed alive,
in spite of the cold.

Worms, snails, woodlice, insects and spiders
stayed alive, too.
Tor and her children could always find
something to eat in the cold forest.

When Tor grew old and died,
many of her children had families of their own.

All through the long cold years,
when the sun hardly shone at all,
Tor's family went on living.

Other small animals were able
to survive in Tor's part of the world.
The frogs, tortoises and lizards hid away
and hibernated when the days grew cold.

Birds had feathers to keep them warm
during the cold grey days and frosty nights.
The birds kept their eggs warm
by sitting on them until they hatched.

But the dinosaurs were not so lucky.

They had no warm fur and no warm feathers.
They were much too big to shelter in holes!
Thousands of dinosaurs died of the cold.

In other parts of the world
small herds of dinosaurs
lived long enough to lay their eggs.
But the eggs did not hatch.
There was not enough sun to keep them warm.

Thousands of plants died
during the cold, frosty nights.

The plant-eating dinosaurs grew hungry.
They needed to eat many leaves to stay alive.
Now they starved to death.

The meat-eating dinosaurs had no food,
and they starved, too.

Tor's family survived, because they were little.
They could always find tiny things to eat.

At long last, the dark clouds of dust
drifted slowly down and settled on the earth.
The warm sun shone again.
Young plants grew from seeds
that had been lying in the ground.

The earth became green again,
but by then there were no dinosaurs left.

The dinosaurs were extinct,
but hundreds of Tor's grandchildren
and great-grandchildren lived on.

In a world without dinosaurs,
the little furry mammals no longer needed
to hide in the dark forests.

The age of dinosaurs was over,
but the age of mammals had come!